$\mathscr{S}$ALADS FOR ALL SEASONS

IMP Limited

CONTENTS

North & Central Europe

3 WAYS WITH POTATO SALAD

SALADS FOR ALL SEASONS

What could be more delicious than a simple salad of mixed leaves dressed in a classic vinaigrette? Here's how to choose and use salad greens.

SHOPPING TIPS

Always buy fresh, crisp salad leaves, with no signs of wilting or discoloration. If something is not available at its best then substitute with another leaf.

STORING LEAVES

Keep salad leaves in the chiller drawer of the fridge, in a sealed plastic bag, and use within 2–5 days. As a rule, the softer the leaf the more quickly it should be eaten. To prepare the salad, pull the leaves off by hand, wash in plenty of cold, running water and dry in a salad spinner or with kitchen paper.

ADDING THE DRESSING

Use a vinaigrette or mayonnaise dressing for your salad leaves. The classic vinaigrette (see page 63) is a mixture of olive oil and wine vinegar, well seasoned with salt, black pepper and mustard; herbs are often added and some people like to include a pinch of sugar. Mayonnaise can be flavoured with garlic, blue cheese, or tomato purée. Add the dressing sparingly — it should cling to the leaves without gathering at the bottom of the bowl — and just before serving so the salad leaves remain crisp.

TIME SAVING TIP

Bags of ready-prepared, mixed leaves, available at most supermarkets, contain a variety of leaves of different tastes, colours and textures. Although relatively expensive, they are cheaper than buying an assortment of whole lettuces, and time-saving as the leaves are ready to use.

HEALTH NOTES

Salad leaves, being fat-free, are a good choice for weight-watchers provided a low fat dressing is used. The darker leaves are more nutritious than light ones. Watercress and spinach, for example, are a good source of folic acid and vitamins A and C; they also supply some iron.

SALAD LEAF SELECTION

The tender leaves of **baby spinach** *(above)* are dark green, soft and velvety. As well as making the perfect garnish, the leaves are particularly versatile as they can be eaten cooked or raw.

Red Oak leaf *(above)* has bronze-tipped jagged leaves and a slightly nutty flavour. It makes an attractive addition to salads and looks good mixed with other leaves. It is also known as Feuille de Chêne and is available in a green variety, **Green Oak leaf.**

Little Gem *(left)* is a small Cos-type lettuce with a sweet, crisp, compact heart. It will keep longer in the fridge than most lettuces.

The large pale leaves of **iceberg** *(leaf shown right)* have become firm favourites of those who love a crunchy texture.

Cos *(above)* is recognised by its long, broad leaves and stout central rib. Crunchy and slightly sweet, it is a favourite for salads and often used with strongly flavoured dressings. Cos is also known as Romaine lettuce.

The small irregular-shaped leaves of **rocket** *(right)* have a distinctive peppery taste becoming more mustard-like as the plant ages.

Radicchio *(above)* belongs to the chicory family. It is notable for its ruby-red leaves with white ribs and is slightly bitter in flavour.

The leaves of **Chinese leaf** *(below)* are long, pale and tightly-wrapped with wide stalks and a sweet mild flavour. They are delicious leaves, raw or in stir-fries.

Lollo Rosso *(left)* has a dense head of frilled leaves, tinged with red. Mix with lighter leaves, or use as a base for salad mixes. **Lollo Biondo** *(above)* is the red version of this lettuce.

CLASSIC WALDORF SALAD

A traditional American salad made from chopped apples, celeriac and walnuts, drizzled with mayonnaise and served on a bed of crisp lettuce — light and delicious.

INGREDIENTS

(Serves 4)

- 1 small celeriac, about 225g/8oz
- 2 tbsp lemon juice
- 2 slightly tart, red-skinned apples, such as Jonathan

FOR THE DRESSING

- 150ml/¼ pint mayonnaise
- pinch of mustard powder
- 3 tbsp sour cream

TO SERVE

- 4-8 large lettuce leaves
- 50g/2oz walnuts

INGREDIENTS TIP

Celeriac is a large, knobbly root vegetable with a strong flavour, similar to that of celery. It is a versatile winter vegetable, good in soups and casseroles as well as salads. Alternatively, you can use 2 sticks of celery.

1 For the dressing, put the mayonnaise, mustard powder and sour cream in a small bowl and mix together with a fork until light, creamy and evenly combined.

2 Place the celeriac on a board and, with a sharp knife or potato peeler, shave off the skin in thick slices, then cut away any 'eyes' or blemishes. Chop the celeriac bulb into segments, then cut into thin slices.

3 Put the celeriac slices into a large mixing bowl and toss with the lemon juice to prevent discolouration (see Cooking tips).

4 Wash the apples, but do not peel them. Remove and discard the core, cut each apple into quarters, and then cut lengthways into fine slices. Add the apple slices to the celeriac in the bowl and toss to combine the ingredients and to coat the apple slices with the lemon juice.

5 Line a serving plate with lettuce leaves and arrange the apple and celeriac slices on top. Drizzle over the mayonnaise mixture. Chop the walnuts roughly and scatter them over the salad. Serve immediately.

Step 1

Step 2

Step 5

Preparation: **15** Min
Per Serving: 464 kcal/1915 kJ;
6g protein; 45g fat; 10g carbohydrate

TYPICALLY NEW YORK

When the luxurious Waldorf-Astoria hotel opened in New York in the 1890s, the chef created this refreshing and novel salad with its unique mix of flavours and textures. Both hotel and salad became legends and retain their popularity to this day.

COOKING TIPS

Like apples, celeriac will discolour once cut unless it is tossed in lemon juice. Lightly blanching the cut celeriac in boiling water for 2 minutes will also prevent it from discolouring • For the best appearance, buy walnut halves and chop them yourself — ready-chopped walnuts tend to look less attractive.

SERVING TIP

Waldorf salad is a favourite for the party buffet, but can also be served as a side-dish with cold cooked meats.

 Best served with a dry sparkling white wine — try one from America or Australia.

WAIKIKI CHICKEN SALAD

USA

This appetizing salad of chicken, celery and peanuts mixes ingredients that are widely used in American-Creole cooking. Juicy tropical fruit adds an exotic flavour.

INGREDIENTS
(Serves 6)

- 3 tbsp sunflower oil
- 6 chicken breasts, skinned and boned
- salt and black pepper
- 1 small fresh pineapple
- 1 papaya
- 5 celery sticks with green leaves
- 50g/2oz unsalted peanuts
- 1 small orange
- 150ml/¼ pint mayonnaise
- ½ tsp Dijon mustard
- 4 kumquats, to garnish

INGREDIENTS TIP

Dijon mustard is medium hot and, because the mustard seeds are dehusked, has a light, creamy-yellow colour. For a more spicy taste substitute the darker Meaux mustard.

1 Heat the oil and fry the chicken breasts on both sides until lightly browned. Cover the pan and leave to cook gently for 10 minutes. Season with salt and pepper, remove from the pan and leave to cool.

Step 1

2 Peel the pineapple, cut lengthways into quarters and remove the thick core and any 'eyes' from the flesh. Cut the quarters into small pieces and put them into a bowl.

Step 2

3 Peel the papaya and halve lengthways. Spoon out the seeds and cut the flesh into cubes. Wash the celery sticks, cut off the leaves and set aside. Cut the sticks diagonally into 6mm/¼in thick slices. Cut the chicken into chunks. Put all the ingredients into the bowl with the pineapple. Chop the peanuts and sprinkle over the salad.

4 Wash the kumquats, cut into slices and scatter over the salad. Grate the rind from the orange and stir into the mayonnaise with the Dijon mustard.

Step 4

5 Spoon the mayonnaise over the salad. Garnish with the celery leaves. Season with salt and pepper and serve immediately.

Preparation: 30 Min
Per Serving: 926 kcal/3835 kJ;
6g protein; 45g fat; 10g carbohydrate

TYPICALLY HAWAIIAN
Sugar cane and pineapple thrive in the fertile volcanic earth of Hawaii and are among its most important sources of income. The island of Lanai, until the 1980s in the hands of the giant Dole Company, is the largest pineapple plantation in the world.

COOKING TIPS

Fresh pineapple is at its peak between September and December. The next best choice is the vacuum-packed pineapple that comes ready-chopped in its own juice — simply drain and add to the ingredients in Step 3. Alternatively, use canned pineapple chunks or pieces in natural juice.

SERVING TIP

Spoon the salad into hollowed-out pineapple halves and serve with warmed vegetable pasties.

Accompany with a cool piña colada — a cocktail made of pineapple juice, rum and coconut cream.

SERVING **TIP** Serve with crisp poppy seed or
sesame seed rolls.

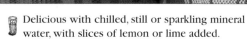 Delicious with chilled, still or sparkling mineral
water, with slices of lemon or lime added.

10

ℐOUTHERN STATES SEAFOOD SALAD

USA

Tasty prawns, tender peas and grated courgettes are flavoured with fresh basil and coated in a light mustard sauce. Served in succulent melon halves, this is the perfect starter.

INGREDIENTS
(Serves 4)

- 275g/10oz courgettes
- 1 tbsp lemon juice
- 150g/5oz fresh garden peas in their shells
- salt
- 250g/9oz cooked, peeled large prawns
- 2 small Charentais melons
- bunch of basil

FOR THE DRESSING
- 3 tbsp white wine vinegar
- salt and white pepper
- 1 tsp herb mustard
- 4 tbsp sunflower oil

INGREDIENTS TIP

A herb mustard, such as Bordeaux with tarragon, adds a tang to the dressing. If you can't find one, use Dijon mustard instead. Frozen peas can be used instead of fresh, but cook them until they are only just tender.

1 Wash the courgettes and cut off the stem. Coarsely grate them and sprinkle with lemon juice to prevent the flesh from discolouring. Cover and set aside.

2 Shell the peas and cook them in boiling salted water for 10 minutes, or until tender. Immediately drain, then refresh by rinsing under cold water to prevent them from cooking further and leave to drain.

3 Put the prawns, grated courgettes and peas in a large mixing bowl.

4 Mix the white wine vinegar, salt, pepper and herb mustard together. Add the oil and beat, with a whisk or fork, to form a creamy salad dressing. Pour it over the salad and toss well to combine the ingredients.

5 Cut the melons in half and scoop out the seeds. Wash and dry the basil. Set a few leaves aside for garnishing and chop the remaining leaves coarsely. Stir into the salad. To serve, spoon the salad into the melon halves and garnish with the reserved basil.

Step 1

Step 2

Step 4

Preparation: **25** Min
Per Serving: 237 kcal/983 kJ;
17g protein; 17g fat; 6g carbohydrate

TYPICALLY SOUTHERN

In the USA, both prawns and shrimps are called shrimps. A traditional favourite in the southern states, they even feature on breakfast menus. The small coastal town of Biloxi, in the state of Mississippi, is known as the shrimp capital of the world.

CAESAR SALAD

USA

Italian cook Caesar Cardini created this salad in the 1920s. The crunchy combination of lettuce, bacon, anchovies and croûtons became a big hit with the Hollywood stars.

INGREDIENTS
(Serves 4)

- 75g/3oz smoked bacon
- 2 slices of white bread
- 3 cloves garlic
- sea or rock salt
- 3 tbsp vegetable oil
- 2 small Cos lettuce hearts
- 4 anchovy fillets
- 50g/2oz Parmesan cheese

FOR THE DRESSING

- 2 eggs
- 4 tbsp olive oil
- 3 tbsp lemon juice
- ½ tsp Worcestershire sauce
- salt and black pepper

INGREDIENTS TIP

As the dressing contains lightly cooked eggs, it should not be served to pregnant women, children, the elderly or those in poor health. Substitute a bought dressing made with pasteurised eggs.

1 Cut the bacon into small cubes. Slice the crust off the bread and cut the bread into 1cm/½in cubes. Peel the garlic and crush 2 cloves together with salt, using a fork.

2 Heat a saucepan, add the bacon and dry-fry until crisp. Remove from the pan and add the oil. Fry the garlic and bread cubes until golden brown. Drain the croûtons well on kitchen paper.

3 Wash and dry the lettuce and tear the leaves. Rinse the anchovies under cold water and chop into small pieces. Coarsely grate the Parmesan cheese.

4 Boil the eggs for 1 minute, then crack and spoon into a bowl. Add the oil, lemon juice and Worcestershire sauce to the eggs and whisk together to make a creamy salad dressing. Season with salt and pepper.

5 Take the remaining garlic clove, cut in half and rub round the inside of a bowl. Put the lettuce, bacon and anchovies in the bowl and toss with the dressing. Top with the garlic croûtons and Parmesan. Serve immediately.

Step 1

Step 4

Step 4

Preparation: **20** Min
Per Serving: 466 kcal/1929 kJ;
14g protein; 43g fat; 7g carbohydrate

TYPICALLY CALIFORNIAN

The Golden State, California, produces a great variety of fruit and vegetables all year round and the Pacific coastline provides fish and shellfish. This bounty from land and sea, influenced by many immigrant cultures, has evolved into a fresh, light, creative cuisine.

COOKING TIPS

It is important that this salad is as fresh as possible, so the dressing should only be mixed, and added, at the last minute • Use an extra-virgin olive oil for the dressing, if you can, as this has the finest flavour. Keep the oil in a cool dark place, but not in the fridge, or it will become cloudy.

SERVING TIP

Serve as a side-dish with grilled chops or sausages.

 A dry Californian Chardonnay is the ideal drink.

CARIBBEAN AVOCADO SALAD

INGREDIENTS
(Serves 4)

- 2 limes
- 2 ripe avocados
- 220g/8oz can palm hearts
- 1 Little Gem lettuce
- 200g/7oz tiger prawns, cooked and shelled

FOR THE DRESSING
- salt and white pepper
- pinch of cayenne pepper
- 3 tbsp sunflower oil

INGREDIENTS TIP
Palm hearts are tender shoots taken from the 'hearts' of palm trees — the snowy white marrow at the base of the palm fronds. They resemble fat white asparagus shoots, and are mostly canned for export. Palm hearts are used both in salads and as a vegetable. They can be replaced by the same amount of canned asparagus.

A speciality of the French island of Martinique, this sumptuous salad combines tender palm hearts, buttery soft avocados, crisp salad leaves and tiger prawns.

1 Halve the limes and squeeze the juice into a bowl. Cut the avocados in half lengthways with a sharp knife, discard the stone and remove the peel.

2 Cut the flesh of the avocados into chunks and put into a bowl. Immediately sprinkle with some of the lime juice to prevent it from discolouring.

3 Drain the palm hearts well. Cut each heart in half lengthways then slice each piece finely with a sharp knife.

4 Separate the lettuce leaves, wash well under running water, then drain. Pat the leaves dry on kitchen paper and use to line a large plate. Scatter over the avocado chunks, sliced palm hearts and the prawns.

5 Make the dressing. Put the remaining lime juice, salt, pepper, cayenne pepper and oil in a bowl and mix together with a whisk or fork. Continue mixing until the salt dissolves and the dressing thickens. Pour the lime and oil dressing over the salad and serve immediately.

Step 1

Step 3

Step 5

Preparation: **20** Min
Per Serving: 258 kcal/1069 kJ;
13g protein; 22g fat; 2g carbohydrate

TYPICALLY CARIBBEAN
The flavours of Africa dominate the Caribbean islands which produce a wide variety of exotic crops due to the successful transplantation of many of the African slaves' favourite ingredients. These include plantain, okra and taro which is similar to yam or sweet potato.

COOKING TIPS

Avocados are ripe when the flesh is soft. To test one, poke a wooden cocktail stick into the pointed end of the avocado — the flesh should have the texture of butter • Hard avocados will ripen more quickly if wrapped in newspaper and left at room temperature for a few days.

SERVING TIP

The warm crunchy bread and rich taste of a garlic baguette make an excellent accompaniment to this dish.

A tropical cocktail of rum and freshly squeezed fruit juices will complement the salad perfectly.

$\mathcal{M}$EXICAN TIJUANA BEAN SALAD

Where would an authentic 'fiesta mexicana' be without a spicy salad of beans and sweetcorn? The fiery taste of green chilli and a zesty lime dressing make this a lively bean dish.

INGREDIENTS
(Serves 4)

- 400g/14oz can kidney beans
- 400g/14oz can cannellini beans or haricot
- 225g/8oz can sweetcorn
- 1 large red pepper
- 1 fresh green chilli
- 1 onion
- 1 clove garlic
- bunch of coriander

FOR THE DRESSING
- 2 limes
- salt and black pepper
- 1 tsp dried oregano
- 4 tbsp sunflower oil

INGREDIENTS TIP

Lime and coriander give many dishes their Mexican flavour. You can substitute with lemon juice and chopped parsley.

1 Thoroughly drain the canned beans and sweetcorn in a colander. Halve the pepper, remove the seeds, wash and pat dry on kitchen paper. Cut into 2cm/¾in long strips. Put in a large bowl together with the sweetcorn and beans.

Step 1

2 Wearing rubber gloves, slice the chilli in half lengthways, remove the seeds and rinse the chilli under cold water. Then, chop into small pieces.

3 Peel the onion and garlic, then finely chop them both. Add the onion and garlic, together with the chopped chilli, to the beans and vegetables.

Step 4

4 Make the dressing by halving the limes, squeezing the juice, then mixing this thoroughly with the salt, pepper, oregano and oil. Use a fork to beat the mixture until thick and creamy. Pour the dressing over the salad, toss and leave to stand for 10 minutes.

5 Wash the coriander and pat dry with kitchen paper. Pluck off the leaves and finely chop them. Mix the coriander into the salad just before serving.

Step 5

Preparation: **30 Min**
Per Serving: 403 kcal/1695 kJ;
15g protein; 17g fat; 51g carbohydrate

TYPICALLY MEXICAN
Compared to our delicate palates, the Mexicans can eat extremely hot dishes. The chilli pepper influences almost every dish in Mexico. There are said to be over 100 varieties indigenous to Mexico itself and they can vary from ¼-12 inches in length.

COOKING TIP

In order to take some of the heat out of chillies, either soak them in salt water for about 10 minutes or peel them. To peel, fry in a saucepan without oil until the skin blisters, then place in a polythene bag immediately and seal. Remove after 10 minutes and peel off the skin under cold running water.

SERVING TIP

This salad is a perfect accompaniment to a juicy steak, tortillas or baked potatoes with a sour cream filling.

 Serve with a chilled Mexican beer such as Sol, or a light beer from the USA.

S ERVING TIP Serve with crispy prawn crackers, which are available from major supermarkets.

 Serve green china tea before and a dry white wine with the salad.

18

INDONESIAN CHICKEN SALAD

INDONESIA

This Indonesian favourite, known as 'gado gado', consists of a piquant peanut dressing poured over a mixture of vegetables. The addition of chicken turns it into a summery main course.

INGREDIENTS
(Serves 4)

- 500g/1lb 2oz chicken breasts, skinned and boned
- 2 tbsp groundnut oil

FOR THE DRESSING

- 2 cloves garlic
- 1 onion
- 2cm/¾in piece root ginger
- 1 tbsp sesame oil
- 125g/4½oz peanut butter
- 90ml/3fl oz water
- salt and black pepper

FOR THE VEGETABLES

- ½ Chinese leaf, about 200g/7oz
- 1 carrot
- 2 celery sticks, with leaves
- 1 tbsp lightly toasted sesame seeds

INGREDIENTS TIP
Sesame oil has a deep amber colour and nutty flavour. Use sparingly as it is very strong.

1 Cut the chicken breasts into small pieces. Heat the oil in a frying pan and stir-fry the chicken, in batches, for about 5 minutes, until lightly browned. Remove from the pan and leave on one side to cool.

2 For the dressing, peel the garlic, onion and ginger. Crush the garlic. Finely chop the onion and grate the ginger. Heat the sesame oil in the frying pan. Fry the ginger and half the onion. Add the garlic, peanut butter and water. Increase the heat and whisk constantly until creamy. Season with salt and pepper, leave to cool.

3 Cut the Chinese leaf into small strips, then wash and leave to drain. Peel and finely grate the carrot. Wash the celery, tear off the green leaves and set aside, cut the stalks into slices.

4 Arrange the vegetables and the rest of the onion on a plate. Add the chicken pieces and pour over the peanut sauce. To serve, scatter with the lightly toasted sesame seeds and garnish with the celery leaves.

Step 1

Step 2

Step 4

Preparation: **35 Min**
Per Serving: 517 kcal/2155 kJ;
36g protein; 38g fat; 8g carbohydrate

TYPICALLY INDONESIAN
A characteristic feature of Indonesian cuisine is its variety of spices, once a much valued commodity. When the Dutch conquered Java and its archipelago at the end of the 18th century, the spices with which they filled their ships were worth their weight in gold.

Asia & The Far East 19

NOODLE AND BEANSPROUT SALAD

VIETNAM

Vietnamese cuisine is an art of subtle spicing. Here shiitake mushrooms, fresh vegetables and an aromatic ginger dressing combine to make an exotic salad.

INGREDIENTS
(Serves 4)

- 100g/4oz vermicelli rice noodles
- 150g/5oz shiitake mushrooms
- 25g/1oz butter
- 1 small red pepper
- 150g/5oz beansprouts
- bunch of coriander

FOR THE DRESSING
- 2cm/¾in piece root ginger
- 3 tbsp soy sauce
- 2 tbsp mild rice vinegar or white wine vinegar
- 2 tbsp sesame oil
- salt and black pepper

INGREDIENTS TIP

You can find shiitake mushrooms in some large supermarkets and Asian grocery stores. Alternatively, use the same amount of oyster or button mushrooms.

1 Put the rice noodles in a bowl. Pour over boiling water and leave for 10 minutes, or according to packet instructions. Drain in a colander and cut into small pieces.

Step 1

2 Clean the mushrooms by rinsing under cold water. Leave to dry or pat dry using kitchen paper, then cut into slices. Melt the butter in a saucepan and fry the mushrooms for 8 minutes over a low heat. Remove with a slotted spoon and leave to cool.

3 Halve the pepper, de-seed and cut into small pieces. Put the beansprouts in a colander, rinse well and leave to drain.

Step 3

4 Pick the coriander leaves from their stalks and finely chop with a sharp knife. Place the leaves in a bowl together with the pepper, beansprouts, noodles and mushrooms.

5 For the dressing, peel and finely grate the ginger. Mix with the soy sauce, vinegar, sesame oil, salt and pepper and whisk well. Pour the dressing over the salad ingredients and toss together. Serve immediately.

Step 5

Preparation: **35** Min
Per Serving: 211 kcal/887 kJ;
6g protein; 13g fat; 21g carbohydrate

TYPICALLY VIETNAMESE
Vietnamese food has been influenced by more than 1000 years of Chinese colonial rule. But unlike Chinese cooking, vegetables served raw such as lettuce, beansprouts, herbs and root vegetables play an important part in Vietnamese cuisine.

COOKING TIP

If you use dried shiitake mushrooms instead of fresh, you need only use 100g/4oz. Soak in boiling water for at least half an hour to re-hydrate them. Drain well before cooking. Whether you use fresh or dried mushrooms, always remove the stems immediately below the cap as these can be tough.

SERVING TIP

Serve this salad in pretty rice bowls and eat with chopsticks. It makes a good accompaniment to chicken.

 Best served with freshly brewed green China tea or warm sake, a Japanese wine made from rice.

3 WAYS WITH VEGETABLE DIPS

Dips can make a delicious treat. Raw vegetables served with different sauces are quick to prepare, healthy and versatile too, plus they make perfect canapés for a party.

PROVENCAL VEGETABLES WITH GARLIC MAYONNAISE

Preparation: **25** Min

FRANCE

(SERVES 4)
- 500g/1lb 2oz small courgettes
- 2 large spring onions
- 2 red peppers

FOR THE DIP
- 4 cloves garlic
- 250ml/9fl oz mayonnaise
- salt and black pepper
- ½ tsp English mustard
- 3 tbsp lemon juice

1 Cut off the stems, then quarter the courgettes lengthways. Wash the spring onions and halve or quarter, depending on size.

2 Wash the peppers, de-seed and cut into 1cm/½in thick strips. Arrange the vegetables on a large plate.

3 Peel the garlic and crush into a bowl. Add the mayonnaise, salt and mustard and mix well until combined.

4 Add the lemon juice and pepper, stir in and serve.

SALAD VEGETABLE

Preparatio

USA

(SERVES 4)
- 2-3 celery sticks
- 3 chicory heads
- 1 small cucumber

FOR THE DIP
- 1 onion
- 2 cloves garlic
- 3 red peppers
- 1 tbsp sunflower oil
- ½-1 tsp chilli powder
- pinch of cayenne pepper
- 1 tsp chopped oregano
- 1 tsp chopped thyme
- bunch of parsley

1 Wash the celery and cut in half lengthways along the sticks. Wash the chicory, trim the base and divide into

VEGETABLES WITH CREAMY BLUE CHEESE DIP

Preparation: **25** Min

ITALY

(SERVES 4)
- 400g/14oz baby carrots
- bunch of spring onions
- 1 small cauliflower
- 2 kohlrabi

FOR THE DIP
- 250g/9oz mascarpone
- 150g/5oz Gorgonzola
- 2 tbsp dry sherry
- salt
- pinch of cayenne pepper
- pinch of paprika
- 25g/1oz chopped pistachios

1 Peel the carrots and quarter lengthways. Wash the spring onions and trim off the dark green leaves. Divide the cauliflower into florets. Peel the kohlrabi and quarter, then cut into slices.

2 Put the mascarpone into a bowl. Dice the Gorgonzola, and add to the bowl with the sherry. Mix together. Season with the salt, cayenne pepper and paprika.

3 Transfer to a small serving bowl. Sprinkle the chopped pistachios on top.

4 Arrange the prepared vegetables on a large plate and serve with the dip.

WITH A FIERY DIP

30 Min Cooking: **10** Min

leaves. Wash and trim the cucumber, cut in half, then cut lengthways into quarters.

2 Peel the onion and finely chop. Peel and crush the garlic. Wash, de-seed and dice the peppers. Heat the oil and fry the onion until lightly browned. Add the peppers, garlic and chilli powder.

3 Cover and cook for 10 minutes, until onion and peppers are tender. Cool slightly.

4 Put the contents of the pan into a blender and purée. Add the cayenne, oregano and thyme. Wash the parsley, finely chop and add to the dip. Serve with the raw vegetables.

$\mathcal{P}$EPPER SALAD WITH SPICY SAUSAGE

HUNGARY

A brightly coloured salad of peppers and onion, tossed with crispy, fried smoked sausage. Garlic and paprika add a real bite to the tangy dressing.

INGREDIENTS
(Serves 4)

- 3 red peppers
- 1 green pepper
- 1 yellow pepper
- 1 onion
- 250g/9oz spicy sausage
- 1 tbsp sunflower oil

FOR THE DRESSING

- ¼ tsp salt
- 2 tbsp red wine vinegar
- 3 tbsp sunflower oil
- 1 clove garlic
- black pepper
- ½ tsp sweet paprika

INGREDIENTS TIP

There are many types of spicy sausage available in local supermarkets these days — find one of a strength to suit your personal taste. If you don't like spicy sausage, try crumbling 250g/9oz goats' cheese into the salad as an alternative.

1 Halve all the peppers lengthways and remove the seeds and white membrane. Wash the peppers thoroughly and pat them dry on kitchen paper. Cut the halves into thin strips and place in a bowl.

2 Peel the onion, cut it into quarters and then into thin slices. Add to the bowl with the pepper and toss them together.

3 Make the dressing. Put the salt and the vinegar in a small bowl and whisk until the salt has dissolved. Add the oil in a thin stream, whisking constantly, until the dressing becomes thick and creamy.

4 Peel the garlic, crush or chop finely and add to the dressing, together with generous pinches of both the black pepper and paprika. Whisk the dressing well, then pour it over the salad. Toss, and leave to stand for about 15 minutes.

5 Cut the spicy sausage into thin slices. Fry in the oil until cooked through and crispy. Add to the pepper salad while still warm, mix together and serve immediately.

Step 1

Step 4

Step 5

Preparation: 25 Min
Per Serving: 345 kcal/1428 kJ;
7g protein; 31g fat; 9g carbohydrate

TYPICALLY HUNGARIAN

The Hungarian national spice is paprika. Red peppers are dried, de-seeded and ground with a large roller made of stone or steel. The amount of seeds added to the ground powder determines how hot the paprika powder will be.

COOKING TIPS

Raw peppers are easier to digest if you briefly blanch them or remove the skin. To skin, bake or grill pepper halves until the skin is charred. Put into a plastic bag and seal. When cold, strip off the skin • If you are in a hurry, stack the pepper halves in layers, then cut them all into slices together.

SERVING TIP

Serve this salad with an assortment of fresh bread rolls or slices of dark rye bread.

 The best wines to accompany this salad are an Hungarian Tokaji Aszu or a white Rioja.

ℬAVARIAN SAUSAGE SALAD

GERMANY

This popular German dish combines mild-flavoured sausages with crunchy, hot radishes. Add a light mustard dressing for a delicious mix of contrasting flavours and textures.

INGREDIENTS

(Serves 4)

- 500g/1lb 2oz German pork sausages
- 1 large mooli weighing about 350g/12oz
- salt
- 100g/4oz small red radishes
- bunch of chives
- 25g/1oz Emmental cheese

FOR THE DRESSING

- 3 tbsp white wine vinegar
- salt and black pepper
- 1 tsp prepared mild German mustard
- 4 tbsp olive oil

INGREDIENTS TIP

A mooli is a large, smooth white radish — though it looks more like a parsnip and is much bigger. It has a fresh, slightly bitter, peppery flavour. Choose one that is firm and unwrinkled.

1 Peel the sausages, halve and slice thinly. Put the slices into a large mixing bowl.

2 Discard any leaves from the mooli, wash thoroughly and grate. Put the grated mooli on a plate, sprinkle over a generous amount of salt and leave to stand for 10 minutes.

3 Trim both ends of the radishes and wash thoroughly. Quarter or cut into eight equal parts, depending on size, and add to the sliced sausages. Wash the chives, chop finely and add to the sausage mix.

4 Put the mooli into a colander and rinse under cold water. Gently squeeze dry with kitchen paper and add to the rest of the ingredients in the bowl.

5 Put the vinegar, salt, pepper, mustard and oil into a small bowl and whisk until creamy. Pour over the salad, toss well to coat, and leave to stand for 10 minutes.

6 Spoon the salad onto a serving plate. Grate the Emmental, sprinkle over the salad and serve.

Step 1

Step 2

Step 3

Preparation: **25** Min
Per Serving: 501 kcal/2072 kJ;
16g protein; 42g fat; 15g carbohydrate

TYPICALLY BAVARIAN

In the summer, spending a sunny afternoon sitting in a shaded beer garden is a popular Bavarian pastime. Many people bring their own food with them, and even their own tablecloth. Favourite snacks include potato salads, pretzels, cheese and cold meats.

COOKING TIPS

Scrub radishes clean with a brush under cold running water and cut away any stringy bits of root • Allow the salad to stand after adding the mustard dressing, so that the dressing can drizzle through and completely coat the ingredients.

SERVING TIP

Line a bread basket with a brightly coloured napkin and fill with salted pretzels.

 A light beer or shandy is traditionally drunk with this Bavarian salad.

SERVING TIP Serve with a mixed green salad, rice or pasta salad, and plenty of crusty bread.

Try an English wine such as a medium dry white from Lamberhurst in Kent.

CORONATION CHICKEN

ENGLAND

This dish was devised by the Cordon Bleu Cookery School for the coronation of Queen Elizabeth II in 1953. It was based on an earlier recipe created for the jubilee of King George V.

INGREDIENTS
(Serves 4)

- 450g/1lb cooked chicken
- 1 onion
- 1 tbsp vegetable or sunflower oil
- 2 tsp hot curry paste
- 2 tsp tomato purée
- 75ml/2½fl oz dry white wine or chicken stock
- 225g/8oz canned apricot halves, drained
- juice of ½ lemon
- 3 tbsp natural yoghurt
- 225ml/8fl oz mayonnaise
- 1 tbsp chopped fresh tarragon or 1 tsp dried
- 75g/3oz seedless green grapes, optional
- tarragon sprigs, to garnish

INGREDIENTS TIP

Apricots canned in fruit juice are best for this recipe as those in syrup are too sweet.

1 Remove the skin from the chicken and cut the flesh into 2.5cm/1in dice. Put in a bowl in the fridge. Peel and chop the onion.

2 Heat the oil in a small saucepan, add the onion and cook for about 5 minutes until soft. Stir in the curry paste, tomato purée and wine or chicken stock. Bring to the boil and simmer for 5 minutes. Remove from the heat and leave to cool.

3 Reserve two or three of the apricot halves for a garnish. Put the rest into a food processor or blender, along with the lemon juice, yoghurt and mayonnaise. Purée together until fairly smooth. Stir in the tarragon and onions.

4 Add the chicken pieces to the apricot mixture and stir until they are well coated in the curried sauce.

5 Spoon the chicken mixture on to a serving plate. Cut the reserved apricot halves into slices and arrange on top of the salad. Garnish with grapes, if using, and tarragon sprigs.

Step 1

Step 2

Step 3

Preparation: **20** Min, plus cooling
Per Serving: 658 kcal/2728 kJ;
30g protein; 54g fat; 11g carbohydrate

TYPICALLY BRITISH

The British tradition of adding spices to dishes dates back to the Middle Ages when cinnamon, ginger and nutmeg were imported from the East. With the colonization of India by the Victorians, curry spices became popular in recipes such as the rice dish, kedgeree.

ℛUSSIAN VEGETABLE SALAD

RUSSIA

A double dressing makes this well-loved salad extra special. The tender, cooked vegetables are tossed first in tangy vinaigrette, allowed to cool, then coated in rich mayonnaise.

INGREDIENTS
(Serves 4)

- 2 carrots
- 1 turnip
- 1 potato
- salt
- 100g/4oz green beans
- 225g/8oz frozen peas

FOR THE DRESSING

- 3 tbsp sunflower oil
- 2 tbsp lemon juice
- 1 tsp Dijon mustard
- salt and black pepper
- 100ml/4fl oz mayonnaise
- 2 tbsp snipped fresh chives

INGREDIENTS TIP
Many other vegetables can be used, such as parsnip, swede, courgettes or celery, but make up a mixture that provides a good contrast of both colour and texture.

1 Peel the carrots, turnip and potato and cut into 1cm/½in dice. Bring a pan of salted water to the boil. Add the vegetables, bring back to the boil and simmer for 5 minutes, or until the vegetables are tender. Drain and place in a bowl.

2 Trim the green beans and cut into 2.5cm/1in lengths. Place in a pan of salted water with the frozen peas, bring to the boil and cook for 3–5 minutes, or until the vegetables are tender. Drain and refresh under cold running water. Add the beans and peas to the diced vegetables in the bowl.

3 Make the dressing by whisking together the sunflower oil, lemon juice, mustard, salt and pepper. Pour it over the vegetables and toss to coat. Leave the salad until the vegetables are cold.

4 Stir the mayonnaise into the vegetables, mixing well so that the ingredients are evenly combined. Spoon the salad into a serving dish. Garnish with the snipped chives and serve immediately.

Step 1

Step 3

Step 4

Preparation: **15** Min, plus cooling
Per Serving: 376 kcal/1556 kJ;
6g protein; 32g fat; 19g carbohydrate

TYPICALLY RUSSIAN
In the days of the tsars the most popular dishes in Central Russia, such as this vegetable salad, were quite rich and heavy. A lighter version is served today as a lunch or supper dish. Cooked fish or chicken are often diced and mixed with the vegetables.

SERVING TIP Serve the salad with cold meats, smoked mackerel, smoked trout, or hard-boiled eggs.

A shot of vodka would be fitting, but this salad is also good with a chilled, dry white wine.

31

FRUITY CHICKEN SALAD

FRANCE

Juicy, sweet nectarines and morello cherries are combined with tender chicken, celery and onions, making a light meal that is perfect for lazy summer days.

INGREDIENTS

(Serves 4)

- 2 tbsp butter
- 575g/1¼lb chicken breasts
- 1 large onion
- 4 celery sticks
- 400g/14oz can morello cherries
- 2 nectarines
- 1 lettuce

FOR THE DRESSING

- 150ml/¼ pint sour cream
- juice of ½ lemon
- salt and black pepper
- pinch of cayenne pepper

INGREDIENTS TIP

Substitute the nectarines with peaches or apricots and the sour cream with crème fraîche or natural yoghurt.

1 Melt the butter in a frying pan. Skin the chicken breasts, then lightly fry on both sides. Cover the pan and leave to cook for a further 10 minutes until cooked through. Remove from the heat and leave to cool.

2 Peel the onion and finely chop. Wash the celery sticks and slice thinly. Drain the cherries and put into a salad bowl with the onion and celery.

3 Dice the chicken breasts. Wash the nectarines and cut into slices, working around the stone. Add half the nectarine slices to the bowl with the chicken.

4 Mix the sour cream and lemon juice together and season with salt, pepper and cayenne pepper. Pour the cream mixture over the ingredients in the bowl and mix well to coat everything evenly.

5 Pull the leaves from the lettuce and rinse under cold water. Spin dry and divide the leaves equally between four serving plates. Spoon the salad on top. Just before serving, arrange the remaining nectarine slices over the salad. Serve immediately.

Step 2

Step 3

Step 5

Preparation: **30** Min
Per Serving: 532 kcal/2225 kJ;
35g protein; 29g fat; 34g carbohydrate

TYPICALLY LORRAINE

Fruit growing is an important industry in the beautiful province of Lorraine in the north east of France. Cherries, apricots, plums, apples and pears are sold in local markets and are also made into delicious fruit brandies and liqueurs.

COOKING TIP

When peeling and stoning the fruit, use nectarines or peaches that are just ripe — not too firm and not too soft. If you use under-ripe fruit the stone will stick to the flesh, making it more difficult to remove. Overripe fruit will squash when you try and twist the two halves apart to remove the stone.

SERVING TIP

The salad could be garnished with chopped chervil leaves. Follow with a platter of cheeses for dessert.

 Serve with a chilled sparkling dry white wine or a light dry white wine, such as Sancerre.

3 WAYS WITH POTATO SALAD

Delicious potato salads are popular in many countries, all of which add different ingredients and dressings to create their own unique dish.

POTATO SALAD WITH AVOCADO AND SWEETCORN

Preparation: **20** Min   Cooking: **25** Min

USA

(SERVES 4)
- 1kg/2¼lb salad potatoes
- salt
- 250g/9oz celery
- 2 avocados
- 1 tbsp lemon juice
- 2 red peppers
- 198g/7oz can sweetcorn

FOR THE DRESSING
- 4 tbsp mayonnaise
- 90ml/3fl oz vegetable stock
- 2 tsp English mustard
- 6 tbsp white wine vinegar
- salt and black pepper
- pinch of cayenne pepper

1 Cook the potatoes in boiling salted water for 20–25 minutes, or until tender, then drain in a colander. Wash the celery and slice thinly. Halve and stone the avocados. Dice the flesh and sprinkle with lemon juice to prevent discolouration.

2 Wash the peppers, de-seed and dice. Drain the sweetcorn. Peel and slice the potatoes. Place two-thirds of the peppers and all the other vegetables on a plate.

3 Mix all the ingredients for the dressing together. Pour over the vegetables, then scatter over the remaining peppers.

POTATO SALA[

Preparatio.

GERMANY

(SERVES 4)
- 1kg/2¼lb salad potatoes
- salt
- 200g/7oz smoked bacon
- 1 tbsp sunflower oil

FOR THE DRESSING
- 200ml/7fl oz chicken or vegetable stock
- 4 tbsp sunflower oil
- 4 tbsp white wine vinegar
- 2 tsp German mustard
- salt and black pepper
- pinch of sugar
- small piece of cucumber
- bunch of spring onions

POTATO SALAD WITH CHEESE AND WALNUTS

Preparation: **25** Min   Cooking: **20** Min   Standing: **20** Min

SWITZERLAND

(SERVES 4)
- 1kg/2¼lb salad potatoes
- salt
- 2 red onions
- small jar of pickled gherkins
- 2 apples
- 1 tbsp lemon juice
- 75g/3oz chopped walnuts
- 200g/7oz Emmental cheese, cut into thick slices
- bunch of chives

FOR THE DRESSING
- 150g/5oz natural yoghurt
- 3 tbsp white wine vinegar
- 3 tbsp sunflower oil
- 2 tsp medium-hot mustard
- salt and black pepper

1 Cook the potatoes in salted water for 20–25 minutes.

2 Peel the onions and chop finely. Drain the gherkins and slice. Cut the apples into quarters and remove the core. Chop into pieces and sprinkle with lemon juice. Put into a bowl with the walnuts.

3 Remove the rind, then dice the cheese. Wash, then chop the chives, and add half to the bowl with the cheese. Drain the potatoes, peel, dice and add to the cheese mixture.

4 Mix the yoghurt, vinegar, sunflower oil, mustard, salt and pepper together and pour over the salad. Sprinkle with the rest of the chives and leave to stand for 20 minutes before serving.

WITH BACON

10 Min   Cooking: **25** Min

1 Cook the potatoes in boiling salted water for 20–25 minutes. Fry the bacon in the oil until crisp.

2 Cut the potatoes into 6mm/¼in thick slices. Put the slices into a bowl.

3 To make the dressing, mix together the stock, oil, vinegar, mustard, salt, pepper and sugar. Pour over the potatoes, then add half the bacon. Leave for 10 minutes.

4 Peel and thinly slice the cucumber and chop the onion. Add to the potatoes. Toss together and scatter the remaining bacon over the top.

TOMATO SALAD JARDINIERE

SOUTHERN FRANCE

The sweetness of fresh vegetables, enhanced by a delicious dressing, contrasts wonderfully with the peppery taste of watercress in this Mediterranean salad.

INGREDIENTS
(Serves 4)

- 275g/10oz small courgettes
- 500g/1lb 2oz cherry tomatoes
- 100g/4oz stoned black or green olives

FOR THE DRESSING
- 3 tbsp white wine vinegar
- salt and white pepper
- 1 tsp Dijon mustard
- 75ml/3fl oz olive oil
- 2 cloves garlic

TO GARNISH
- large bunch of watercress

INGREDIENTS TIP

Substitute watercress with rocket. Both have a strong, peppery flavour, or for a milder leaf, use baby spinach.

1 Wash the courgettes and remove the stalk. Cut them into quarters lengthways and then chop each quarter into small chunks.

2 Wash the tomatoes, remove the stalk, and cut into quarters. Put into a large salad bowl with the courgettes.

3 For the dressing put the vinegar, salt, pepper and mustard together in a bowl and mix. Whisk in the oil, a little at a time, until it combines with the other ingredients to make a creamy dressing.

4 Peel the garlic, crush and stir into the dressing. Pour the dressing over the tomatoes and courgettes, then add the olives. Mix the ingredients thoroughly.

5 Wash the watercress in plenty of cold water, tear the leaves from the tough stalks and pat dry with kitchen paper. Add the leaves to the salad and mix them in carefully, to avoid bruising them. Serve.

Step 1

Step 2

Step 4

Preparation: **25 Min**
Per Serving: 230 kcal/947 kJ;
3g protein; 22g fat; 5g carbohydrate

TYPICALLY PROVENÇAL

In Provence, in the south of France, olives grow in abundance — there may be as many as 30 varieties to choose from in the outdoor markets. The small town of Nyons, considered to be the centre of olive production, has an olive mill and museum to visit.

COOKING TIP

Watercress should be used when it is really fresh.
Keep bunches up-ended in a bowl of water in the
refrigerator as the sprigs absorb moisture through
their leaves. Vacuum packs of ready-washed
watercress should not be opened until you are ready
to use them or the leaves will turn yellow.

SERVING TIP

This salad makes an excellent
side dish for a leg of lamb coated
with fragrant herbs and roasted.

 Serve with a light French red wine such as
Beaujolais, or a rosé such as Côtes du Rhône.

$\mathscr{S}$ALADE NICOISE

A classic salad from the south of France made with green beans, tomatoes, anchovies and tuna. Add black olives for a truly authentic appearance.

INGREDIENTS
(Serves 4)

- 500g/1lb 2oz green beans
- salt
- 250g/9oz tomatoes
- 50g/2oz can anchovy fillets
- 2 onions
- 200g/7oz can tuna

FOR THE DRESSING

- 4 tbsp white wine or sherry vinegar
- 1 tsp English mustard
- salt and white pepper
- 6 tbsp olive oil

INGREDIENTS TIP

Try to use green beans which have been picked when young and tender. They can be substituted with mange tout or runner beans. If you are using runner beans, you might have to trim the tough, stringy edges, cut them into shorter lengths and cook for slightly longer.

1 Wash the green beans, then top and tail them. Cut them into pieces about 4cm/1½in in length.

2 Bring a little salted water to the boil in a small saucepan. Add the beans and cook for 5–10 minutes, or until the beans are just tender. Drain in a colander and rinse well under cold water to refresh the beans and stop them from cooking further.

Step 1

3 Wash the tomatoes, remove the stalks, and cut into wedges. Rinse the anchovy fillets under cold running water. Pat them dry carefully with kitchen paper and cut each fillet lengthways in half.

4 Peel the onions and slice them into thin rings. Drain the tuna in a sieve, then flake into small pieces using a fork.

Step 4

5 Lightly mix together the beans, tomatoes, anchovies, sliced onions and flaked tuna in a large salad bowl.

6 For the dressing, whisk the vinegar, mustard, salt, pepper and olive oil until combined and creamy. Pour over the salad ingredients and serve immediately.

Step 5

Preparation: **20 Min**
Per Serving: 346 kcal/1433 kJ;
19g protein; 27g fat; 7g carbohydrate

TYPICALLY PROVENÇAL

Niçoise is the French term used to describe dishes using tomatoes, green beans, olive oil and other ingredients typical of the area of southern France around Nice. Olives have been cultivated here and pressed for their oil since Roman times.

COOKING TIP

To prepare in advance, follow the recipe to the end
of Step 5. Make up the dressing as directed in Step 6
but do not add the dressing to the salad. Instead store
the salad and the dressing separately in sealed plastic
containers in the fridge for up to 24 hours. Toss the
salad with the dressing just before serving.

SERVING TIP

Salade niçoise is an ideal dish for a picnic.
Arrange it on lettuce leaves with olives and
hard-boiled eggs.

 The perfect drink to complement the salad is a
Côtes de Provence rosé wine.

SERVING TIP Serve with crusty French bread cut
into large chunks and spread with butter.

Delicious with a white wine from south-west France,
such as Jurançon.

40

$\mathscr{B}$ROCCOLI SALAD WITH ROQUEFORT DRESSING

SOUTHERN FRANCE

Broccoli is delicious cooked until just tender and served cold in salads. Here it is combined with sweet red peppers and coated in a wonderfully seasoned Roquefort dressing.

INGREDIENTS

(Serves 4)

- 575g/1¼lb broccoli
- salt
- 2 red peppers
- 2 tbsp sunflower seeds

FOR THE DRESSING

- 100g/4oz Roquefort cheese
- 4 tbsp sour cream
- 2 tbsp white wine vinegar
- salt and black pepper
- pinch of ground nutmeg
- bunch of parsley

INGREDIENTS TIP

Sour cream is made by adding a 'souring' culture to single cream, which thickens it and gives it a slightly sharp flavour. Natural yoghurt or crème fraîche can replace sour cream in many recipes.

1 Divide the broccoli into florets. Peel the thick stalks and slice. Cook the florets and slices of stalk in salted, boiling water for 5–8 minutes. Pour into a colander, refresh by rinsing under cold water, and leave to drain thoroughly.

2 Wash the peppers, halve and remove the seeds and the white membranes. Cut the pepper flesh into small dice. Put them in a large salad bowl with the cooled broccoli pieces and toss together.

3 Using a fork, mash the Roquefort in a small bowl. Add the sour cream and white wine vinegar and mix well together. Season with salt, pepper and nutmeg.

4 Arrange the salad on four serving plates. Wash the parsley, chop the leaves and mix with the dressing. Drizzle the dressing equally over the salads.

5 Dry-fry the sunflower seeds in a heavy-based frying pan over a high heat for about 30 seconds, stirring continuously, until lightly coloured. Scatter the warm seeds over the salads and serve immediately.

Step 1

Step 3

Step 5

Preparation: **20** Min
Per Serving: 214 kcal/887 kJ
13g protein; 16g fat; 5g carbohydrate

TYPICALLY FRENCH

Roquefort, a blue cheese made from ewes' milk, is one of France's oldest cheeses and is only made in the village of Roquefort near the Cévennes mountains. The mountains provide ideal grazing land for sheep and the cheese is matured in the village's limestone caves.

$\mathcal{T}$USCAN TOMATO SALAD

ITALY

This Italian salad features fresh, sun-ripened tomatoes and peppers, dressed up with finely chopped sweet onion and aromatic basil, in a top quality dressing.

INGREDIENTS
(Serves 4)

- 200g/7oz crusty white loaf
- 3 tbsp red wine vinegar
- 1 tsp balsamic vinegar
- 500g/1lb 2oz tomatoes
- 1 mild onion
- 1 small yellow pepper
- 1 small red pepper
- 2 tbsp capers, optional
- 2 cloves garlic
- bunch of basil

FOR THE DRESSING
- 2 tbsp red wine vinegar
- salt and black pepper
- 4 tbsp olive oil

INGREDIENTS TIP

It is important to choose really ripe tomatoes so this salad has a full flavour. Buy fresh basil if available, but dried will do, otherwise use only ½ teaspoon and whisk into the dressing.

1 Remove the crusts from the bread, slice and cut into 2cm/¾in cubes. Put the bread cubes into a bowl. Mix the red wine vinegar, balsamic vinegar and 2 tablespoons of water together. Pour the mixture over the diced bread and toss well to coat. Cover and leave to stand for at least 15 minutes.

2 Wash the tomatoes and remove the stalks. Slice, then chop the flesh into small pieces and put into a bowl. Peel the onion and chop finely. Wash, de-seed and dice the peppers. Add the onion, peppers and capers, if using, to the tomatoes. Peel the garlic and crush into the vegetable mixture.

Step 2

3 To make the dressing, mix the red wine vinegar, salt, pepper and the olive oil together. Reserve a sprig of basil. Rinse, pat dry and coarsely shred the rest and add to the tomato mixture.

Step 3

4 Add the marinated bread to the tomato mixture. Pour over the salad dressing, toss and leave to stand for about 5 minutes. Garnish with the basil sprig and serve.

Step 4

Preparation: **35** Min
Per Serving: 274 kcal/1146kJ;
5g protein; 16g fat; 29g carbohydrate

TYPICALLY TUSCAN

Tuscan cooking is based on simple country dishes made with the finest quality, fresh ingredients. Locally produced olive oil, a variety of fresh herbs, home-baked bread and rolls, and fresh vegetables form the basis of many Tuscan dishes.

COOKING TIPS

The drier the bread is, the easier it will soak up the dressing. It is better to slice the bread and leave it out to dry the day before making the salad • Capers are usually quite vinegary. It's a good idea to soak them in milk or water prior to using. The capers left in the jar should always be kept submerged in liquid.

SERVING TIP

Serve with Italian ciabatta slices as a starter, or as an accompaniment to grilled fish or lamb chops.

A young Chianti Classico, from the heart of Tuscany, is the perfect wine for this salad.

Tomato and Mozzarella Salad

ITALY

The creamy white mozzarella, red tomatoes and green basil of this salad mirror the national colours of Italy. The 'insalata tricolore' as it is known has become an international favourite.

INGREDIENTS

(Serves 4)

- 3 x 125g/4½oz packets mozzarella cheese
- 575g/1¼lb ripe large tomatoes
- salt and black pepper
- bunch of fresh basil
- 90ml/3fl oz olive oil

INGREDIENTS TIP

Italian mozzarella, made from cows' milk, is available from supermarkets in individually wrapped 125g/4½oz balls or loose from the deli counter. You can also buy it ready-grated for pizzas, or in bite-size balls for appetizers, but choose the larger size for this salad. Genuine mozzarella, made from buffalo milk, is mainly produced in the Campania and Latium regions.

1 Unwrap the packets of mozzarella cheese, leave to drain in a colander, then cut into 6mm/¼in thick slices.

2 Wash and dry the tomatoes and remove the stalks. Cut each tomato into 6mm/¼in thick slices, using a serrated knife.

3 Arrange the slices of tomato and mozzarella on a large serving dish, alternating each slice of tomato with a slice of mozzarella. Overlap the slices evenly.

4 Season the tomato and the mozzarella slices with salt and a generous amount of freshly ground black pepper.

5 Briefly rinse the basil under cold running water, shake well and pat dry with kitchen paper. Tear off whole leaves of the basil and tuck them between the slices of tomato and mozzarella.

6 Carefully drizzle the olive oil evenly over the salad. Grind over more black pepper, if liked, and serve immediately.

Step 1

Step 3

Step 5

Preparation: **20** Min
Per Serving: 306 kcal/1266 kJ;
4g protein; 30g fat; 6g carbohydrate

TYPICALLY CAPRIAN

This classic, three-coloured summer salad originates from the Italian island of Capri, just off the coast of Naples. Tomatoes and basil grow in abundance on the isle and the salad tastes especially delicious when both are freshly picked.

COOKING TIPS

If you prefer tomatoes skinned, slit the skin of each, put in a bowl, cover with boiling water and leave for 30 seconds. Drain, then rinse under cold water so the skin can be removed easily • Basil is sold in growing pots in supermarkets. Larger leaves can be pungent so use smaller sprigs if you prefer a milder flavour.

SERVING TIP

Serve with toasted Italian white bread, sprinkled with olive oil, and a bowl of stoned black olives.

The salad is complemented by a dry white wine, such as Gallestro or Pinot Grigio.

SERVING TIP Serve with bread or new potatoes for a light meal or on its own as a starter.

 Serve with a light Italian white wine, such as Prosecco or Trebbiano.

$\mathscr{S}$EAFOOD SALAD

ITALY

Squid, prawns and mussels combined with sun-ripened tomatoes and herbs in a pleasantly piquant dressing make a superbly flavoured seafood salad.

INGREDIENTS
(Serves 4)

- 2 lemons
- salt
- 275g/10oz prepared small squid
- 2 tomatoes
- 1 onion
- bunch of flat-leaved parsley
- bunch of basil
- 2 cloves garlic
- 150g/5oz cooked mussels, bottled or fresh
- 200g/7oz peeled prawns

FOR THE DRESSING

- salt and black pepper
- ½ tbsp balsamic vinegar or red wine vinegar
- 4 tbsp olive oil

INGREDIENTS TIP
Balsamic vinegar has a syrupy consistency and strong, concentrated flavour, so a little goes a long way.

1 Squeeze the lemons. Add 1 tablespoon lemon juice to 1 litre/1¾ pint salted water and bring to the boil. Cut the squid into 6mm/¼in rings, add to the water and simmer for 6–8 minutes. Leave to cool in the water.

2 Blanch the tomatoes by placing in a bowl and covering with hot water. Drain, peel, de-seed, then cut the flesh into cubes. Peel the onion, finely chop and put into a bowl together with the tomatoes.

3 Rinse the parsley and basil, tear off the sprigs and leaves, reserving a parsley sprig for garnish. Pat dry, finely chop and add the herbs to the bowl. Peel the garlic, crush and add to the mixture.

4 Drain the squid in a colander. Drain the mussels, if necessary, and add to the bowl together with the prawns and the squid.

5 Mix the rest of the lemon juice with salt and pepper, the vinegar and olive oil. Pour the dressing over the salad, mix well, cover and put into the fridge for the flavours to combine — about 15 minutes. Garnish with the reserved sprig of parsley and serve.

Step 3

Step 4

Step 5

Preparation: 45 Min
Per Serving 274 kcal/1141 kJ;
29g protein; 17g fat; 1g carbohydrate

TYPICALLY NORTH ITALIAN
In the fresh fish markets of Genoa and Venice, stall holders and customers haggle over the price of fish and seafood brought in by fishing boats. Each year in May, many markets hold a huge street party at which visitors flock to sample the cooked catches.

PASTA SALAD WITH TUNA MAYONNAISE

ITALY

Pasta tossed with colourful vegetables and dressed with creamy tuna mayonnaise makes an easy, yet satisfying, salad either served on its own or as a buffet dish.

INGREDIENTS
(Serves 4)

- 225g/8oz pasta, such as spirali, penne or shells
- 1 tbsp olive oil
- 200g/7oz can tuna
- juice of ½–1 lemon
- 2 tbsp capers or 1 tbsp white wine vinegar
- 150ml/¼ pint mayonnaise
- black pepper
- ½ red pepper
- 5cm/2in piece cucumber
- 75g/3oz canned sweetcorn, drained
- 2 hard-boiled eggs
- basil leaves

INGREDIENTS TIP

The capers add a vinegary flavour to the mayonnaise and stop it being too rich. White wine vinegar is a good substitute for capers.

1 Cook the pasta in a large saucepan of lightly salted boiling water for 6–7 minutes (or according to the packet instructions) until al dente — just firm to the bite, but cooked through. Drain well in a colander. Place the pasta in a large mixing bowl and toss well with the olive oil.

2 Drain the tuna and use a fork to roughly break it into flakes. Put the tuna into a blender or food processor. Add the lemon juice to taste, capers or wine vinegar, and mayonnaise and blend together until smooth and creamy. Add to the pasta, season with black pepper, and stir together until the ingredients are evenly mixed.

Step 2

3 De-seed the pepper. Wash and pat dry on kitchen paper, then finely dice. Finely dice the cucumber without removing the skin. Add the pepper, cucumber and sweetcorn to the pasta and toss together. Spoon into a serving dish.

Step 3

4 Remove the shell from the hard-boiled eggs and cut into quarters. Arrange the wedges decoratively over the salad and garnish with small basil leaves.

Step 3

Preparation 15 Min
Per Serving 673 kcal/2817 kJ;
25g protein; 41g fat; 55g carbohydrate

TYPICALLY ITALIAN

Tuna mayonnaise features in one of Italy's most famous recipes, Vitello Tonnato where it is mixed with cold chopped veal. Anchovies are added as well as capers to the mayonnaise to counteract its richness and the dish is garnished with black olives and lemon wedges.

SERVING TIP Accompany with a salad of bitter
leaves, such as radicchio, rocket and watercress.

Serve with a crisp dry Italian white wine, such as
Pinot Grigio or Frascati.

ℳARINATED MUSHROOMS

ITALY

Thinly sliced mushrooms soak up the delicious flavours of a marinade made from chillies, garlic, lemon juice and olive oil to make an appetizing starter.

INGREDIENTS

(Serves 4)

- 500g/1lb 2oz mushrooms
- bunch of flat-leaved parsley

FOR THE MARINADE

- 2 lemons
- 5 tbsp olive oil
- salt and black pepper
- pinch of sugar
- 4 cloves garlic
- 1 fresh red chilli

INGREDIENTS TIP

As the flavour and texture of mushrooms deteriorate quickly, really fresh ones are needed to enjoy this salad at its best. Mushrooms shouldn't need peeling, just wipe or rinse away any compost that is clinging to them and trim the end off the stalk.

1 For the marinade, squeeze the lemons and pour the juice into a bowl. Add the olive oil, salt, pepper and sugar. Whisk the ingredients until they are thoroughly combined. Peel and crush the garlic and add this to the marinade.

2 Halve the chilli lengthways and de-seed. Rinse under cold water, then cut into very thin slices and add to the marinade. Wash your hands if not wearing rubber gloves when handling the chilli.

3 Wipe the mushrooms clean with damp kitchen paper. Trim the stalks. Cut the mushrooms into thin slices and add to the marinade. Toss gently to coat.

4 Rinse the parsley and tear off the sprigs. Reserve one sprig for each serving. Finely chop the rest and add to the mushrooms. Cover the bowl and put into the fridge. Leave to marinate for at least 5 hours – or overnight if possible.

5 To serve, spoon onto individual plates and garnish each with a sprig of parsley.

Step 3

Step 3

Step 4

Preparation: 30 Min
Marinating: 5 Hours
Per Serving: 185 kcal/762 kJ;
2g protein; 19g fat; 1g carbohydrate

TYPICALLY ITALIAN

Italians enjoy eating in a relaxed, informal way and most celebration meals start with a selection of antipasti, or starters, placed on the table for guests to help themselves. Typical antipasti include grilled and marinated vegetables, and simple salads.

COOKING TIPS

Use an egg cutter to slice mushrooms. It will save time and they will all be the same thickness • The longer the mushrooms are left to marinate, the better they will taste. However, they should be removed from the fridge about 1 hour before serving to allow them to return to room temperature.

SERVING TIP

Serve with bruschetta, toasted Italian bread drizzled with garlic and olive oil and topped with tomatoes and basil.

 Serve with a dry Prosecco from Venice or a spritzer — dry white wine and soda water.

SPANISH TUNA SALAD WITH ASPARAGUS

SPAIN

Luxorious, tender green asparagus are used in this recipe in place of the more traditional white. It's served with tuna in a slightly sharp, oil and vinegar dressing.

INGREDIENTS
(Serves 4)

- 500g/1lb 2oz fresh asparagus or 2 x 400g/14oz cans asparagus
- salt
- 500g/1lb 2oz tomatoes
- Cos lettuce heart
- 1 Spanish onion
- 200g/7oz can tuna in oil
- 4 canned anchovy fillets
- bunch of flat-leaved parsley
- 12 pimiento-stuffed green olives

FOR THE DRESSING
- 5 tbsp olive oil
- 4 tbsp red wine vinegar
- salt and black pepper

INGREDIENTS TIP

The season for home-grown asparagus is short — May and June — but imported ones are available at other times of the year. Alternatively, you can use canned asparagus.

1 If using fresh asparagus, peel and cut off the woody end. Cook in plenty of boiling salted water for 15 minutes, or until tender, then drain in a colander. If using canned asparagus, drain carefully and set aside.

2 Wash the tomatoes, discard the stalks and cut them into eight wedges. Thickly slice the Cos lettuce, wash and drain well.

3 Peel the onion, cut into quarters and slice thinly. Drain the tuna and coarsely flake with a fork. Rinse the anchovy fillets under cold water and cut them into small pieces. Wash the parsley, tear off the sprigs, pat dry and finely chop.

4 For the dressing, pour the olive oil and the red wine vinegar into a large bowl. Add the salt and pepper and whisk until the salt has dissolved. Divide the asparagus between four serving plates and sprinkle it lightly with some of the dressing.

5 Mix the tuna, chopped tomatoes, lettuce, chopped onion, anchovies, olives and parsley together and toss in the remaining dressing. Serve with the asparagus.

Step 1

Step 2

Step 3

Preparation: **20** Min
Per Serving: 472 kcal/1961 kJ;
35g protein; 34g fat; 6g carbohydrate

TYPICALLY SPANISH
Vegetables, rice, fruit and fish are abundant in southern Spain and feature in many dishes, from gazpacho (iced tomato soup) and paella to simple starters and salads based on asparagus, onions and tomatoes. Sherry is drunk with meals in the south of the country.

COOKING TIP

Lettuce leaves will stay fresher for longer if they are first washed and dried, and then placed in a plastic freezer bag. Loosely tie or seal the bag and keep it in the vegetable compartment at the bottom of the fridge. Herbs will also stay fresh for several days if stored in the same way.

SERVING TIP

This salad makes an excellent partner for the typically Spanish potato omelette Tortilla de Patatas.

This dish is ideally served with a light Spanish red wine such as Valdepeñas.

53

ANDALUSIAN ORANGE SALAD

SPAIN

Whether it's winter or summer, this vitamin-rich salad, prepared with tender spinach leaves, juicy oranges and a fragrant thyme dressing, always tastes delicious.

INGREDIENTS

(Serves 4)

- 250g/9oz fresh baby spinach leaves
- 4 oranges
- 100g/4oz stoned black olives

FOR THE DRESSING

- juice of ½ lemon
- salt and black pepper
- pinch of sugar
- 4 tbsp olive oil
- few sprigs of fresh thyme or 1 tsp dried

INGREDIENTS TIP

Substitute the oranges with two pink grapefruit and the olives with cucumber slices. Extra-virgin olive oil is deep green with a rich, full flavour, while golden-coloured varieties have a lighter taste. Use whichever you prefer.

1 Pick over the spinach leaves, discarding any that have yellowing edges. If necessary, cut off any tough stems. Rinse the leaves in a small amount of cold water and drain well in a colander.

2 For the dressing, put the lemon juice, salt, pepper and sugar for the dressing into a large bowl and mix well. Whisk in the olive oil and continue whisking until the salt and sugar dissolve. If using fresh thyme, rinse well, shake dry, then tear off the leaves. Add the thyme to the dressing.

3 Rinse one orange under hot water and dry thoroughly. Finely grate half of the rind and stir this into the dressing. Peel the oranges, taking care to remove all of the white pith. Free the orange segments from their membranes using a small, sharp knife and remove any pips. Cut any large segments in half.

4 When ready to serve the salad, arrange the spinach, oranges and olives on a serving plate, pour the dressing over them and serve immediately.

Step 1

Step 2

Step 3

Preparation: **35** Min

Per Serving: 236 kcal/977 kJ;
4g protein; 18g fat; 15g carbohydrate

TYPICALLY ANDALUSIAN

The Arabs introduced orange trees to the coastal strips of the southern Spanish province of Andalusia. The Moorish kings grew the decorative plants in their gardens. Consequently, oranges were regarded as a luxury by Spaniards for many years.

COOKING TIPS

When separating the orange segments, work over a
plate to catch the juice from the orange. Mix this into
the dressing with the lemon juice — it will mellow
the sharpness of the lemon • As spinach leaves wilt
quickly after the dressing is added, combine the
salad ingredients just before serving.

SERVING TIP

This salad is often served as an
accompaniment to lamb kebabs. Add
crunch by sprinkling with pine nuts.

Serve with a medium dry Amontillado sherry or a
dry white Rioja wine.

GREEK SALAD

This traditional rustic salad is an ideal snack for hot summer days. The combination of crunchy vegetables, feta cheese and oregano needs only crusty bread to go with it.

INGREDIENTS
(Serves 4)

- 1 cucumber
- 1 green pepper
- 500g/1lb 2oz tomatoes
- 1 red onion
- 200g/7oz feta cheese
- 100g/4oz black olives

FOR THE DRESSING

- 3 tbsp wine vinegar
- pinch of salt
- 5 tbsp olive oil
- black pepper
- 1 tsp fresh oregano
  or ½ tsp dried

INGREDIENTS TIP

Red onions are used in many Mediterranean dishes and have a mild, almost sweet flavour. Their attractive colour also makes them particularly suitable for salads.

1 Peel the cucumber, halve lengthways and scrape out the seeds with a spoon. Cut the halves into 1cm/½in thick slices.

2 Halve the pepper, de-seed and cut into strips. Wash the tomatoes, remove the stalks, then cut into eight equal wedges.

3 Peel the onion, slice in half, cut into rings and halve the rings. Put all the chopped vegetables into a big bowl.

4 Dice the feta cheese or crumble it with your fingers. Remove the stones from the olives if necessary. Add the cheese and olives to the ingredients in the bowl.

5 For the dressing, stir together the wine vinegar and salt until the salt has completely dissolved. Whisk in the oil in a thin stream. Continue whisking until the dressing is creamy. Season with plenty of black pepper and add the oregano.

6 Pour the dressing over the ingredients in the bowl and leave to marinate for about 1 hour before serving.

Step 1

Step 4

Step 5

Preparation: **30** Min Marinating: 1 Hour
Per Serving: 343 kcal/1416 kJ;
10g protein; 32g fat; 5g carbohydrate

TYPICALLY GREEK

The countryside around Kalamata, in the Peloponnese region of Greece, is the most important area for the cultivation of Greek olives. The olives are pickled in brine and eaten on their own, or as part of a dish, and are also pressed to produce a high-quality oil.

COOKING TIPS

Strong goats' or ewes' milk cheese will become
milder in flavour if marinated in milk for a day
before using • Fresh oregano leaves just need to be
pulled off their stalks. If you use dried oregano, rub it
between your fingers to release its full aroma.

SERVING TIP

Serve this salad as a starter, with bread
or rolls as a snack, or as a side-dish with
Souvlaki (chargrilled meat kebabs).

Serve with Retsina, the Greek wine with a
distinctive resinous flavour.

57

SERVING TIP Serve with pitta or another flat bread as an appetizer, or as a side-dish with lamb.

A yoghurt drink spiced with pepper and cumin, or a light rosé wine enhances the salad's flavours.

MOROCCAN VEGETABLE SALAD

MOROCCO

Mint gives a zing to this light and crunchy salad, prepared with tomatoes, peppers, onions and cucumbers, while the cumin adds a warm, aromatic spiciness.

INGREDIENTS
(Serves 4)

- 3 tomatoes, about 400g/14oz in total
- 1 cucumber
- 1 large white onion
- 1 small red pepper
- 1 small green pepper
- bunch of flat-leaved parsley
- bunch of mint

FOR THE DRESSING
- 5 tbsp lemon juice
- salt and black pepper
- pinch of ground cumin
- 5 tbsp sunflower oil

INGREDIENTS TIP

Fresh mint is best for this salad as dried mint has very little aroma. A hardy herb, fresh mint is available all year round and can be bought growing in pots or packed in bags from supermarkets.

1 Remove the tomato stalks, wash and, using a sharp knife, score the skin lightly with criss-crossed lines. Place the tomatoes in a bowl, cover them with boiling water for 30 seconds, then drain and peel off the skin. Halve, de-seed and cut the tomato flesh into small cubes.

2 Peel the cucumber and halve lengthways. Scrape out the seeds with a teaspoon. Cut each half into small cubes.

3 Peel the onion and chop finely. Halve the peppers, de-seed and cut out the stalks and white pith. Wash the pepper halves and cut into small cubes.

4 Rinse the parsley and mint and shake dry. Tear off the sprigs and leaves and coarsely chop. Discard any tough stalks.

5 For the dressing, thoroughly mix the lemon juice, salt, pepper, cumin and oil in a large bowl. Gently toss the vegetables and chopped herbs in the dressing. Cover the bowl, put into the fridge and leave to marinate for about 1 hour before serving.

Step 1

Step 4

Step 5

Preparation: **30** Min Marinating: **1** Hour
Per Serving: 202 kcal/833 kJ;
1g protein; 20g fat; 4g carbohydrate

TYPICALLY MOROCCAN

The Moroccans serve something minty and cooling with almost every main course to counteract the hot, spicy dishes they love so much. Fresh mint is widely used to flavour tea and other drinks, as well as in salads and meat marinades.

COUSCOUS SALAD

MOROCCO

INGREDIENTS
(Serves 4)

- 225g/8oz couscous
- 200g/7oz tomatoes
- 1 baby cucumber
- bunch of spring onions
- bunch of parsley
- bunch of mint

FOR THE DRESSING

- 2 lemons
- salt and black pepper
- pinch of ground cumin
- 4 tbsp olive oil

INGREDIENTS TIP

Couscous is made by moistening grains of semolina, forming them into tiny pellets and coating with wheatflour. It is sold in all large super-markets, usually alongside the dried beans and pulses.

This popular Moroccan dish is based on couscous, a type of semolina, which is mixed with chopped salad vegetables and a variety of aromatic fresh herbs.

1 Soak the couscous in a bowl of water, or steam it, according to the manufacturer's instructions on the packet.

2 Meanwhile, cut the tomatoes in half and chop into small dice. Peel the cucumber, halve lengthways and spoon out the seeds. Slice the cucumber and cut into small chunks. Clean and trim the spring onions and cut into thin rings. Put all of these ingredients into a large salad bowl.

Step 1

3 Rinse the parsley and mint and carefully pat dry with kitchen paper. Set aside some of the sprigs of mint for garnishing. Finely chop the parsley and the remaining mint leaves. Add to the tomatoes, cucumber and spring onions in the bowl, together with the soaked or steamed couscous.

Step 3

4 Halve the lemons and squeeze the juice into a small bowl. Add the salt, pepper, cumin and olive oil to the bowl, then beat the ingredients together using a whisk or fork. Pour the dressing over the salad, mix well and leave to stand for 15 minutes. Garnish with the mint sprigs and serve.

Step 4

Preparation: **30** Min, plus soaking
Marinating: **15** Min
Per Serving: 207 kcal/856 kJ;
2g protein; 16g fat; 15g carbohydrate

TYPICALLY MOROCCAN

A traditional way to eat couscous in Morocco is to mix it with meats, spices and chick peas and cook it in an earthenware pot called a tagine. The Moroccans love hot dishes and each town has its own market selling an array of fiery and aromatic spices.

COOKING TIP

Most couscous sold in supermarkets is pre-cooked so it just needs soaking or steaming briefly before serving or adding to a recipe. Be sure to read the packet instructions first as brands vary, and some varieties sold in ethnic shops may take longer to prepare and may also need cooking before use.

SERVING TIP

Serve with a little harissa, a fiery chilli paste. It is available from larger supermarkets and ethnic shops.

 Best served with fruit juices, or tea with slices of lemon added rather than milk.

DICTIONARY OF TERMS

This glossary will guide you through some of the terms and ingredients you may come across in making salads.

Beansprouts are crisp, delicately flavoured shoots sprouted from dried soya or mung beans. Sold fresh in supermarkets, they should be kept in the fridge and rinsed well before use. Use to give your salads and coleslaws an extra crunch.

Capers are the unopened flower buds of a Mediterranean plant that grows like a creeper. The buds are pickled in a vinegar brine. They give a sharp flavour when added to other salad ingredients or blended with a rich dressing, such as mayonnaise.

Crisping involves wrapping dried salad leaves in kitchen paper and refrigerating them for several hours to crisp.

Croûtons are small cubes of bread, fried, baked or toasted, until crisp and golden. When shallow frying, flavour by adding garlic cloves to the pan. (Garlic croûtons are a vital ingredient in Caesar Salad.)

Drying watery salad is important as soggy leaves can cause stored greens to deteriorate quickly. Always drain leaves well in a colander and pat dry using kitchen paper.

Ginger is the knobbly, underground root of a south-east Asian plant with a hot, spicy flavour. Peel and grate or finely chop the fresh root and add to salad dressings or marinades. Jars of ready-grated fresh ginger are available on the herb and spice shelves from supermarkets. Ginger is especially good in oriental salads, particularly those with chicken and seafood.

Mayonnaise is a dressing made from egg yolks, oil, and wine vinegar or lemon juice, plus seasoning. Fresh mayonnaise contains raw egg yolks, so should not be eaten by infants, pregnant women, the elderly or anyone in poor health. Commercially prepared, bottled mayonnaise is

OILS AND VINEGAR

Make your own dressing by mixing different oils and adding your favourite vinegar.

TYPES OF OIL
GROUNDNUT – *also known as peanut oil. The clear oil is extracted from the roasted nuts and has a mild flavour.*

OLIVE – *pressed from fresh olives, extra-virgin is considered the finest and fruitiest of the olive oils. Lighter flavoured, golden varieties are also available, so choose the oil best suited to your salad ingredients or mix extra-virgin with a milder variety.*

SESAME – *deep amber in colour with a strong nutty flavour. Use sparingly or it will dominate other ingredients.*

SUNFLOWER – *mild flavoured and pale yellow in colour. Good for all types of salad dressing.*

TYPES OF VINEGAR
BALSAMIC – *a dark, concentrated vinegar produced in Italy from fermented grape juice. Use it in small quantities as it is very strongly flavoured.*

CIDER – *made from apple pulp, it is mild and slightly sweet.*

RICE – *very mild with low acidity, made from fermented sake, or rice wine. Used in Chinese and Japanese cooking.*

WINE – *produced from either red or white wine, which determines its colour. Pleasantly pungent, it can be flavoured with garlic, chilli or herbs.*

made with pasteurized egg and therefore does not present a health risk. It can be plain or flavoured, full-fat or reduced-calorie. Refrigerate on opening.

Mustard seeds are classified as a spice. They can be left whole for grain mustards or ground and sold as powder. Mustard is available ready-mixed in tubes, jars or stone pots. English mustard is bright yellow and hot; French, such as Dijon, is darker and less pungent, while American and German mustards tend to be milder.

Nutmeg is the hard brown seed of the nutmeg fruit from a south-east Asian tree. The outer, web-like, coating is a spice called mace. Nutmeg is sold whole, or ground. It loses its flavour quickly once ground so if possible, buy a whole nutmeg and grate what you need. Use sparingly in dressings — it goes well with spinach salads.

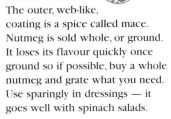

Refreshing vegetables for salads, particularly green ones, is necessary to set their colour and prevent them cooking any further. First rinse them under cold water after cooking. Then drain well before dressing them.

Soy Sauce is a light or dark brown sauce with a sweet/savoury taste, made from boiled,

---

---

fermented soya beans. Soy sauce is used in oriental recipes and in sauces, dressings and dips.

Vinaigrette is the classic French dressing for salad leaves. To make 125ml/4fl oz vinaigrette dressing, whisk 2 tbsp white wine vinegar or lemon juice with 1 tsp Dijon mustard and season to taste. Gradually whisk in 6 tbsp olive oil until blended and thickened.

Worcestershire Sauce is a spicy sauce, produced from vinegar, anchovies, treacle, tamarind, chillies, shallots and spices, which dates back to Victorian days. Worcestershire sauce has a pungent flavour so only a few drops are needed to add piquancy and interest to a sauce, dip or dressing. Add to oriental-style salads based on fish, chicken, seafood or shredded vegetables.

INDEX

Acknowledgements

Picture Credits
All cover and recipe pictures:
International Masters Publishers BV/International Masters Publishers Ltd
Michael Brauner, Food Photography Eising, Karl Adamson, Dorothee
Gödert, Neil Mersh, Jonathan Reed, Peter Rees, Manuel Schnell
With special thanks to David Mellor for supplying props

Agency pictures:
Introduction Fotex: Thornton, page 4/5 Robert Harding.
Pictures for the Typically Sections: Bavaria: PP, page 32
Anthony Blake, Page 29, 30, 44, 48, 50; Cephas: Prousst, Page 36
Rock, page 41; Eising: Jakobi, page 56; Focus: Butlaud, page 50
Hussenot, page 38; Satore, page 12; Silvester, page 52
Fotex: Berke, page 8; Robert Harding: Layda, page 6
Woolfitt, page 16; IFA Bilderteam: Aberham, page 26
Seidenberger, page 59; Spence, page 14
Image Bank: Edmunds, page 20; Lockyer, page 54
Rakke, page 11; Impact: Achache, page 47; Cormack, page 24
Panos Pictures: Dugast, page 60; Tony Stone: Chesley, page 19
Telegraph Colour Library: Noton, page 42

Measuring Ingredients
Tsp – teaspoon, Tbsp – tablespoon
Teaspoons and tablespoons are level and measured using standard
measuring spoons.
Follow either metric or imperial measurements and don't mix the two.

© International Masters Publishers BV/International Masters Publishers Ltd
MCMXCVIII
Reproduced by Studio One Origination, London, UK
Printed in Italy by Mondadori